When thought, feeling and motion collide, reality bends.

THE TRISCENDENT WAY

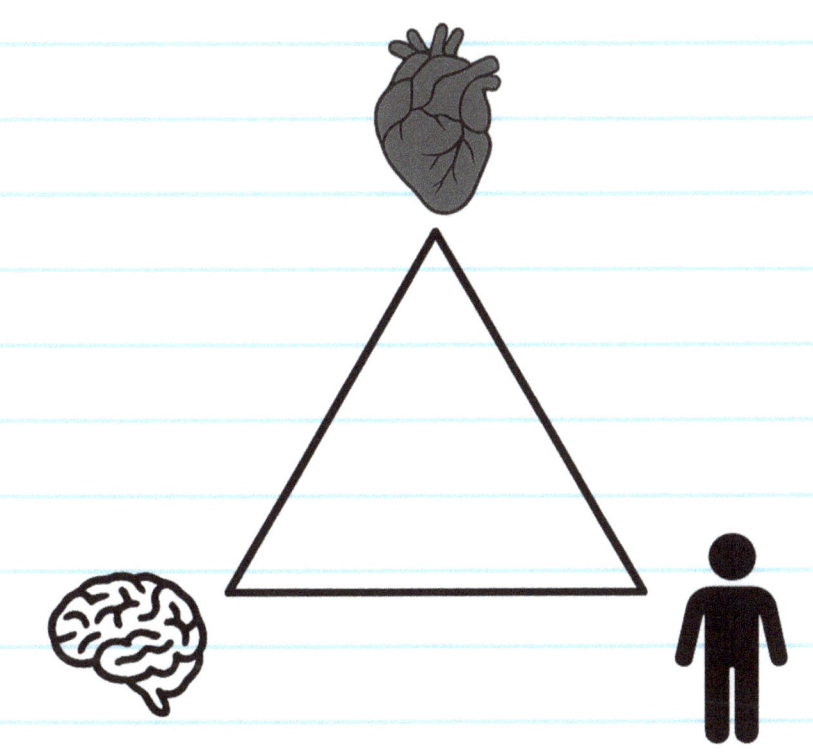

WRITTEN BY MIYA B. ALLEN, ESQ.

THE TRISCENDENT WAY
Copyright © 2025 Miya B. Allen, Esq.
All rights reserved.

Published by Triscendent Press
An imprint of NEW Media, Inc.

No part of this book may be reproduced, stored in a retrieval system, or transmitted in any form or by any means including electronic, mechanical, photocopying, recording, or otherwise without prior written permission from the publisher, except for brief quotations used in reviews or scholarly work.

ISBN (Paperback): 979-8-9940716-0-1
ISBN (Hardcover): 979-8-9940716-1-8

Printed in the United States of America.

For more information, visit: Triscendent.com

TABLE OF CONTENTS

Introduction 2

The Law of One 6

The Way of the Tao 8

The Quantum Leap 9

The Triscendent Circuit 11

The Triscendent Circuit Chart 12

The Brain 13

The Heart 21

The Body 31

Closing 41

About the Author 42

References 43

INTRODUCTION
Quantum Leaping and Coherence

Quantum leaping means making a big jump in your reality... skipping the slow, step-by-step path and shifting into a completely new version of yourself or your life.

It's based on the idea that there are many possible realities (like websites on the internet), and your thoughts, emotions, and focus decide which one you "tune in" to.

Manifestation is how you make that leap real. When your thoughts (mind), feelings (heart), and actions (body) all match the reality you want, you start attracting experiences that fit that version of you. So instead of chasing change, you become the change and reality catches up.

THE BRAIN 🧠

The Remote of Reality.

The brain functions like a remote, tuning consciousness to different frequencies of experience and directly controlling the body. It holds access to the combined consciousness of the past, present and future, what mystics call the Akashic Records, or the collective subconscious of "all that is."

When your thoughts are coherent, your imagination, focus, and beliefs don't just observe reality, they select it.

THE HEART 🫀 The Frequency Amplifier

The heart's aura is more than poetic; it's measurable. Each heartbeat emits an electromagnetic field that extends several feet beyond the body.

This field changes with emotion: love and gratitude produce smooth, coherent waves, while fear and anger create erratic ones.

Your heart becomes both instrument and transmitter, harmonizing your frequency with others and with Source itself. We are living incarnations of all incarnations, the same consciousness viewed from countless perspectives. The only difference between us is our angle of experience. Through the heart, we remember that connection.

Source: McCraty & Childre, 2010; McCraty et al., 2009; McCraty, 2017

THE BODY 👤 The Vehicle

The body grounds the unseen into matter. It is how vibration becomes form. The vessel that anchors mind and heart into action. Through movement, breath, and presence, the body translates energy into reality.

The body is how we take action towards the dreams that the brain projects, the body is how we carry out the frequency of the heart.

However, the body is in direct contact with the trauma of the physical world and it doesn't forget. Those without coherence fall mercy to the body's negative impulses.

Now, let's review foundational principles to bring the brain, body and heart together.

The Law of One and The Path Of Integration

Though they lived in different times and places, Jesus Christ and The Buddha (Siddhartha Gautama) taught nearly the same heart truth: that heaven or enlightenment isn't a distant realm, but a state of being found within.

Jesus Christ said: "The kingdom of God is within you."
The Buddha said: "Look within, you are the light of the world."

Both turned away from material wealth to live in peace, compassion, and service, revealing that the real battle is not against others, but within. Between fear and love, illusion and truth...

The Law Of One and The Path Of Integration (Continued).

When viewed together, Jesus Christ represents divine love awakening the heart, while The Buddha represents divine wisdom awakening the mind.

Together, they mirror the same Oneness, The Law of One, expressed in different languages.

The Law of One teaches that everything, people, animals, stars, and space itself, is part of one great whole.

To live in alignment with this Oneness, one must move from separation to connection, from selfishness to service.

🌊 The Way of the Tao

(Inspired by Lao Tzu, Tao Te Ching, 6th century BCE)

The Tao (pronounced Dao) means "The Way."
It's not a religion, it's the natural flow of life itself.

The Tao teaches that everything in existence, light and dark, stillness and motion, joy and pain, is part of one balanced whole. When we stop fighting what is and learn to move with life instead of against it, we return to harmony.

Like water, the Tao doesn't force, it flows. It finds its path through patience and softness, shaping mountains without struggle.

No control, no excess, but alignment. Trust the rhythm of nature. In Taoist terms, wisdom is effortless balance, living so that the mind, heart, and body move as one with The Way.

THE QUANTUM LEAP

Now that the foundational principles of oneness and flow are in place, let's focus on coherence.

Quantum leaping is about collapsing separation. It is not a miracle, but a shift in frequency alignment. When your brain, heart, and body operate in coherence, physical reality bends around your focus. You no longer chase, you resonate.

The universe responds to coherence like a song finding its key. Once in tune, reality harmonizes around you. Time bends. Synchronicities appear. Healing accelerates.

THE QUANTUM LEAP
(Continued)

Stop manifesting from need and start magnetizing from wholeness. The moment your heart overrides doubt, your brain stops buffering, and your body releases resistance, reality will catch up to your frequency.

You are the signal, the instrument and all that is becoming aware of itself.
This is the Triscendent Way.
A daily practice, a gentle science, a return to Oneness.

The Triscendent Circuit

When systems are fragmented, life is experienced in lag time. The body reacts before the brain understands; the brain imagines before the heart agrees; the heart becomes heavy or empty without proper release.

When practiced in sequence, these elements form a self-healing circuit:
Body acts → Brain projects → Heart aligns → Body acts again

Your consciousness stops fragmenting and the same energy that once scattered you now sustains you. Conscious feedback made visible.

This is the Triscendent Circuit.

Triscendent Circuit Chart

MODE	WHAT IT SOLVES	HOW IT REBALANCES
DREAM (BRAIN)	BURNOUT, ANXIETY, CREATIVE BLOCK, DISTRACTION, DISCONNECTION FROM INTUITION	Reconnects to the universal field, updates your internal software. Reopens flow, imagination, and access to subconscious guidance.
REFLECTION (HEART)	EMOTIONAL SUPPRESSION, SHAME, NUMBNESS, INDECISION, ENERGETIC IMBALANCE, GUILT	Brings stillness, forgiveness, and emotional clarity. Restores coherence and raises your vibration to match your dream world.
MISSION (BODY)	DISCONNECTION, PROCRASTINATION, LACK OF STRUCTURE, OVERWHELM, NUMBNESS, SURVIVAL MODE	Converts physical reaction into intentional motion and presence. Restores rhythm, discipline, and embodied confidence.

THE BRAIN
Alignment and Misalignment

The brain is the remote. It tunes your reality through focus and perception and controls your body. Every thought is a frequency, every belief a signal.

Alignment: focus, awareness, precision, direction, inspiration

Misalignment: anxiety, depression, mental disorder

Imagination and Creativity.

Albert Einstein once said, "Imagination is more important than knowledge." Over a century later, neuroscience confirms it. Daydreaming activates more brain regions than problem-solving, engaging memory, vision, and emotion in what's called the Default Mode Network, the brain's creative web.

This network allows ideas to form connections that logic alone can't reach, turning quiet moments into bursts of innovation. Structured daydreaming can raise creative problem-solving by 41%, while also boosting empathy and emotional intelligence.

Sources: Mason et al., Science (2007); Christoff et al., PNAS (2009); Immordino-Yang et al., Perspectives on Psychological Science (2012); Harvard Gazette (2012); Isaacson, Einstein: His Life and Universe (2007).

Neuroplasticity and Repetition

Your brain doesn't distinguish between good or bad, only what you repeat.

Every thought and behavior creates neural pathways that deepen with practice. This is why habits, whether uplifting or destructive, become automatic. The same mechanism that wires stress or distraction can also wire focus, gratitude, and resilience.

Sources: Doidge (2007) The Brain That Changes Itself; Pascual-Leone et al., Annual Review of Neuroscience (2005); Draganski et al., Nature (2004); Davidson & Lutz, IEEE Signal Processing Magazine (2008).

Resilience Circuits

Resilience is not fixed, it's trainable.

The anterior mid-cingulate cortex (aMCC) helps the brain decide when to push through challenge. Each successful effort strengthens these circuits through neuroplasticity. <u>Avoidance weakens them.</u>

Mindfulness, goal-setting, and controlled stress exposure fortify this network, building the mental stamina to transform difficulty into growth.

Sources: Frontiers in Psychiatry (2023); Nature Neuroscience (2016); Neuroplasticity Research Review (2024).

The Cost of Negativity.

Chronic complaining or repetitive negative thinking releases stress hormones and rewires the brain for threat detection.

Even a single minute of venting raises cortisol, weakens memory circuits, and reinforces anxious bias. Yet gratitude and mindful language reverses this pattern, increasing hippocampal activity and emotional stability.

Sources: Sapolsky (2004); McEwen Nature Reviews Neuroscience (2007); Lupien Nature Reviews Neuroscience (2009); Fox Frontiers in Psychology (2015); Marchant et al., Alzheimers & Dementia (2020); Sáiz-Vázquez et al., BMC Psychiatry (2025).

The Observer Effect and "Quantum Luck"

In 2019, Oxford physicists demonstrated that expectation alters outcomes: particles behaved differently when observers anticipated a result.

This supports the observer-coherence effect: confidence shapes perception, attention, and opportunity.

People who believe in their luck literally notice more chances, translating quantum probability into real-world success.

The evidence is clear: Consciousness, focus, and belief determine which of many possible realities you experience.

Sources: Oxford Quantum Experiments (2019); Zurich Cognitive Probability Study (2020).

Mastering The Brain: Dream Mode

Dream Mode Function:
Creator, Translator of Solutions. Your brain is half hardware, half wifi.

The subconscious connects to the infinite internet of intelligence of the past, present, and future, while the conscious mind is simply the webpage you're viewing right now.

Dream mode is where visualization becomes rehearsal, and imagination becomes architecture. When you visualize you are not pretending. You're opening a data stream between the reality you're in and the one you're choosing.

Mastering The Brain: Dream Mode
(Continued)

In dream mode, you practice "positive delusion," seeing yourself where you want to be until the nervous system agrees. The frontal lobe lights up, translating emotion into instruction.

Through imagination, focus, and positive delusion you rewrite your code. Dream mode teaches you how to use your mind as a portal instead of a prison to listen to the messages of your body without becoming them.
It's not escaping the world, it's coding it.

THE HEART
Alignment and Misalignment

The heart is an amplifier. It magnifies whatever energy you feed it. When aligned, your heart broadcasts coherence: clear, harmonious signals that guide your intuition and relationships. When misaligned, static fills the channel, distorting both inner and outer communication.

Alignment: honesty, forgiveness, acceptance, gratitude, intuition

Misalignment: hate, regret, lies, ungratefulness, avoidance, isolation

The Heart's Electromagnetic Field

Your heart doesn't just beat, it broadcasts. Every heartbeat sends an electromagnetic wave that extends several feet beyond your body, measurable with sensitive instruments like magnetometers.

Scientists at the HeartMath Institute discovered that the heart's electromagnetic field is the strongest rhythmic signal produced by the human body. Over 60 times stronger than the brain's electrical field.

The Heart's Electromagnetic Field
(Continued)

The Heart's field shifts with your emotions:

- Feelings of love, gratitude, and peace create smooth, coherent patterns.
- Fear, anger, or stress create jagged, chaotic waves.

What's extraordinary is that your heart's field can influence others. When you're calm, centered and loving, people around you unconsciously sync with that coherence. Their heart rhythms begin to harmonize with yours.

The Heart's Electromagnetic Field
(Continued)

Ancient traditions called this influential field your aura or life force; modern science calls it electromagnetic resonance.

Either way, it's the same truth:
The heart is not confined to the body. It's a transmitter of energy, connection, and emotional information that bridges us all.

Sources:
- McCraty, R. & Childre, D. (2010). Coherence: Bridging Personal, Social, and Global Health. HeartMath Institute.
- McCraty, R. et al. (2009). The Energetic Heart: Bioelectromagnetic Communication Within and Between People.
- McCraty, R. (2017). Heart-Brain Neurodynamics: The Making of Emotions. Global Advances in Health and Medicine.

The Heart and Consciousness

Whether spiritual or secular, studies show that prayer and meditation reshape the brain toward emotional control, compassion, and clarity.

In spiritual terms, this is Christ Consciousness: love awakening the heart.

In Buddhist terms, it is mindfulness: awareness dissolving illusion.

Both activate the same inner circuitry: the merging of heart frequency and brain rhythm into coherence.

Sources: Newberg & Waldman, How God Changes Your Brain (2009); Tang et al., Nature Reviews Neuroscience (2015); Brewer et al., Psychiatry Research (2011).

CBT to Aid Heart Coherence

Cognitive Behavioral Therapy (CBT) helps you identify and rewrite the thought patterns shaping your reality.

CBT helps the heart by translating emotional chaos into understanding. It gives your feelings language and helps you see the stories behind them, gently rewiring how your heart and mind communicate.

As you write the following prompts in a dedicated journal, you will begin to release emotional tension stored in the body. Repeat this exercise once per week.

After each session, rest and drink plenty of water. This is no easy task.

CBT to Aid Heart Coherence
(Continued)

1. Emotion you want to heal → describe this emotion.

2. Where do you feel it in your body? What is the sensation? Intensity 1–10 (10 being the worst pain you've ever felt).

3. Bridge first and worst: When was the first time you ever felt this emotion? The worst time?

4. What did these experiences make you believe about yourself?

5. What are the things you have lost, or will continue to lose, if you don't heal from this?

6. I validate that these things have happened to me, and my hope for myself is: _____.

7. Who are the people that can help me?

Grateful Child Mediation

This meditation returns you to the simplest and purest state of being. The child within you who exists only in presence, never in pursuit.

Sit or lie comfortably, allowing your breath to soften. In your heart, invite the presence of a trusted parent. Not of flesh, but of spirit.

This parent asks nothing of you, needs nothing from you, and gives endlessly when you are the same. There is no goal here. No lesson. No desire. Only the wish to share this moment.

Allow yourself to be a child again. A grateful child who remembers what it means to just be. Sit with this parent, who is not separate but Oneness itself. The love that remains when desire ends.

Mastering the Heart: Reflection Mode

Reflection Mode Function:
The heart is not just a feeling center, it is the control room, the only organ capable of overriding both body and brain.

When you enter Reflection Mode, you slow down enough to meet yourself and access the field that unites all energy.

Here, coherence is found in the gentle space between breath and thought, achieved through meditation and forgiveness.

Mastering the Heart: Reflection Mode
(Continued)

In reflection mode, you integrate everything you've done and dreamed, fine-tuning your personal frequency to become a vibrational match for your dreams.

Spending time in your heart is like sitting with a trusted parent with no wants and no needs, simply existing in their presence. Here, self and source merge in quiet understanding.

This is how you convert pain into wisdom and emotion into energy.

Reflection Mode doesn't demand. It receives.

THE BODY
Alignment and Misalignment

The body is the vehicle carrying the mind's direction and heart's vibration into the physical world. When aligned, movement and stillness exist in harmony. When misaligned, the body mirrors environments and choices that betray us.

Alignment: health, wellness, flow, harmony, balance, energy, responsiveness

Misalignment: illness, dangerous environments, self-betrayal, distress, fatigue

The Body as a Messenger of the Past

Pain, illness, or exhaustion are not enemies; they are messages.

When we treat physical symptoms not as punishment, but as communication from our energy system, healing begins.

The physical world, including your body, is a recording of past thoughts, emotions, and beliefs. Every cell reflects yesterday's alignment between your brain and heart.

The Body as a Messenger of the Past
(Continued)

Not every message deserves our full attention. The art lies in filtering what the body says and distinguishing between signals that require healing and echoes of outdated programming.

When you identify the difference, you free your nervous system from replaying old frequencies. The body no longer dictates your future based on your past.

The Body as a Messenger of the Past
(Continued)

When you make the quiet choice to realign, by recognizing the difference between healing and programing, your frequency shifts. Since reality mirrors vibration, change can happen in the blink of an eye.

This is quantum leaping through embodiment: translating awareness into motion, transforming pain into power and stepping into a physical reality that matches the vibration of your desires.

The Importance of Movement

Movement and breath connect the brain and heart to the body's rhythm anchoring Oneness in daily life.

The body is designed to move energy, not store it. Every time you move, you translate unseen emotion into flow.

Stillness is sacred, but stagnation is not. When the body becomes motionless for too long, energy clogs the circuits between heart and brain, clouding intuition and dulling awareness.

The Importance of Movement
(Continued)

Every repetition, every conscious action, trains the nervous system to respond with grace instead of fear.

Through mindful physical practice (exercise, dance, yoga, walking, or any form of embodied awareness) the body becomes the translator, turning coherence into motion.

Movement is the physical language of manifestation. It tells your subconscious, "I am here. I am alive. I am capable."

Sources: Charney & Southwick, Time (2015); Yale Stress Center (2018); Ahead App Summary (2022).

Daily Movement Sequence Chart

Duration: 7 minutes, no equipment needed.
Purpose: Activate flow between brain, heart, body through breath and awareness.

1. Grounding Breathing (1 minute)	Stand with feet hip-width apart. Inhale deeply through the nose for 4 counts, expanding your belly. Hold for 2 counts. Exhale through the mouth for 6 counts. Feel your weight settle into your feet.
2. Energy Sweep (1 minute)	Sweep your arms up overhead in an inhale, imaging light rising through your spine. Exhale as you bring your hands down through your centerline, clearing your energy feild. Repeat 5-6 times.
3. Heart Expansion (2 minutes)	Place one hand over your heart, the other over your abdomen. With each inhale, gently open your chest; with each exhale, release your shoulders down. Visualize your heart field expanding several feet around you.
4. Dynamic Flow (2 minutes)	Rotate wrists, ankles and neck slowly. Roll your shoulders, sway side to side or move freely to soft music. Let your movement be intuitive, no choreography, just release.
5. Still Integration (1 minute)	Sit or stand in stillness. Close your eyes. Feel your heartbeat syncing with your breath. Whisper internally: "I am in motion, I am in flow."

The Power of Action

Quantum leaping isn't magic without action. Fantasizing about your goals without acting on them keeps your energy suspended in potential. A dream without grounding.

Action is the bridge between vibration and quantum leaping. Each step, no matter how small, signals to your subconscious that you are ready to receive.

The universe mirrors not your wishes, but your willingness.

The Power of Action
(Continued)

When you move toward your vision, you collapse the gap between imagination and experience. Your body becomes the evidence of belief.

Every aligned action, from a workout to a written plan, from a phone call to an act of service, reshapes the field around you.

Momentum builds coherence.
Movement proves faith.
Dreaming creates the path.
Doing makes it real.

Mastering the Body: Mission Mode

Mission Mode Function:

Receiver and Reactor. Mission Mode restores clarity through movement, repetition, and physical awareness. This is the way you show up when no one's watching.

Your body is not the problem, it is the messenger. Every tension, ache, or pattern is your environment speaking. When ignored, these messages pile up and crash the system.

When the body stops looping the problem, it begins transmitting the solution. It tells your subconscious: "I can be trusted with the dream."

Every task is a sacred act grounding you into the material world.

THANK YOU

By reading this, you've initiated the quantum leap. The journey of brain, heart and body coherence is a return to your natural alignment with Oneness. The next step is to read this again and begin applying.

Remember: Your Brain is the remote, tuning your focus. Your Heart is the amplifier, translating emotion. Your Body is the vehicle, grounding energy into motion.

When these three move in harmony, you stop chasing reality and start creating it.

For more information, visit Triscendent.com

ABOUT THE AUTHOR

Miya Allen, Esq. is a filmmaker and attorney whose life is proof that alignment can turn any start into possibility.

A first-generation college graduate who once dropped out of high school, she built a professional life entirely on her own terms, moving from surviving to thriving.

With a background in Film and Religion, Miya spent a decade in entertainment before traveling the world as a remote attorney.

Everything she's accomplished was born from the same philosophy she teaches: when the brain, heart, and body move in coherence, reality realigns to meet you there.

REFERENCES

Ahead App. (2022). Ahead app summary. Ahead Health Technologies.

Brewer, J. A., Worhunsky, P. D., Gray, J. R., Tang, Y.-Y., Weber, J., & Kober, H. (2011). Meditation experience is associated with differences in default mode network activity and connectivity. Psychiatry Research: Neuroimaging, 191(1), 36–43. https://doi.org/10.1016/j.pscychresns.2010.08.006

Charney, D. S., & Southwick, S. M. (2015, June 24). Resilience: The science of mastering life's greatest challenges. Time Magazine; see also Yale Stress Center. (2018). Stress and resilience research overview. Yale School of Medicine.

Christoff, K., Gordon, A. M., Smallwood, J., Smith, R., & Schooler, J. W. (2009). Experience sampling during fMRI reveals default network and executive system contributions to mind wandering. Proceedings of the National Academy of Sciences, 106(21), 8719–8724. https://doi.org/10.1073/pnas.0900234106

Davidson, R. J., & Lutz, A. (2008). Buddha's brain: Neuroplasticity and meditation. IEEE Signal Processing Magazine, 25(1), 176–174. https://doi.org/10.1109/MSP.2008.4431873

Doidge, N. (2007). The brain that changes itself: Stories of personal triumph from the frontiers of brain science. Viking Press.

Draganski, B., Gaser, C., Busch, V., Schuierer, G., Bogdahn, U., & May, A. (2004). Neuroplasticity: Changes in grey matter induced by training. Nature, 427(6972), 311–312. https://doi.org/10.1038/427311a

Fox, K. C. R., et al. (2015). Functional neuroanatomy of meditation: A review and meta-analysis of 78 functional neuroimaging investigations. Frontiers in Psychology, 6, 763. https://doi.org/10.3389/fpsyg.2015.00763

Frontiers in Psychiatry. (2023). Special issue on neurocognitive integration and mental health. Frontiers Media SA.

Harvard Gazette. (2012, January 24). Eight weeks to a better brain. Harvard University.

Immordino-Yang, M. H., Christodoulou, J. A., & Singh, V. (2012). Rest is not idleness: Implications of the brain's default mode for human development and education. Perspectives on Psychological Science, 7(4), 352–364. https://doi.org/10.1177/1745691612447308

Isaacson, W. (2007). Einstein: His life and universe. Simon & Schuster.

Lupien, S. J., McEwen, B. S., Gunnar, M. R., & Heim, C. (2009). Effects of stress throughout the lifespan on the brain, behaviour, and cognition. Nature Reviews Neuroscience, 10(6), 434–445. https://doi.org/10.1038/nrn2639

REFERENCES

Marchant, N. L., et al. (2020). Mindfulness, cognitive decline, and Alzheimer's disease: A review. Alzheimer's & Dementia, 16(10), 1474–1483. https://doi.org/10.1002/alz.12164

Mason, M. F., et al. (2007). Wandering minds: The default network and stimulus-independent thought. Science, 315(5810), 393–395. https://doi.org/10.1126/science.1131295

McCraty, R. (2017). Heart–brain neurodynamics: The making of emotions. Global Advances in Health and Medicine, 6(1), 4–14. https://doi.org/10.7453/gahmj.2017.006

McCraty, R., & Childre, D. (2010). Coherence: Bridging personal, social, and global health. Alternative Therapies in Health and Medicine, 16(4), 10–24.

McCraty, R., Atkinson, M., & Tomasino, D. (2009). The energetic heart: Bioelectromagnetic communication within and between people. HeartMath Research Center, Institute of HeartMath.

McEwen, B. S. (2007). Physiology and neurobiology of stress and adaptation: Central role of the brain. Nature Reviews Neuroscience, 10(6), 431–445. https://doi.org/10.1038/nrn2648

Nature Neuroscience. (2016). Special issue: Brain plasticity and adaptive learning. Nature Publishing Group.

Neuroplasticity Research Review. (2024). Emerging directions in neural adaptability. International Neuroscience Consortium.

Newberg, A., & Waldman, M. R. (2009). How God changes your brain: Breakthrough findings from a leading neuroscientist. Ballantine Books.

Oxford Quantum Experiments. (2019). Quantum cognition and probability fields. University of Oxford Press.

Pascual-Leone, A., Amedi, A., Fregni, F., & Merabet, L. B. (2005). The plastic human brain cortex. Annual Review of Neuroscience, 28, 377–401. https://doi.org/10.1146/annurev.neuro.27.070203.144216

Sáiz-Vázquez, O., et al. (2025). Neuroplastic effects of mindfulness and psychedelics on affective disorders. BMC Psychiatry, 25(1), 41. https://doi.org/10.1186/s12888-025-0541-2

Sapolsky, R. M. (2004). Why zebras don't get ulcers: The acclaimed guide to stress, stress-related diseases, and coping. Henry Holt and Company.

Tang, Y.-Y., Hölzel, B. K., & Posner, M. I. (2015). The neuroscience of mindfulness meditation. Nature Reviews Neuroscience, 16(4), 213–225. https://doi.org/10.1038/nrn3916

Zurich Cognitive Probability Study. (2020). Quantum probability and cognition: Zurich cognitive probability study. University of Zurich Cognitive Science Institute.

www.ingramcontent.com/pod-product-compliance
Lightning Source LLC
Chambersburg PA
CBHW051326110526

44582CB00003B/58